A Magnificent Monument of Mural Art –
The Story of Princes Dock

by

Adrian Jarvis

Illustrations by Samantha Ball
Photographic work by David Flower

ERRATUM

An unfortunate error has led to the illustration for page 37 being printed on page 41 and vice versa. The captions are on the correct pages.

NATIONAL MUSEUMS & GALLERIES
· ON MERSEYSIDE ·

First published 1991 by Merseyside Port Folios,
1 & 3 Grove Road, Rock Ferry,
Birkenhead, Wirral, Merseyside L42 3XS.

Merseyside Port Folios is the joint publishing imprint of the
National Museums and Galleries on Merseyside and Countyvise
Limited.

Copyright © The Trustees of the National Museums and Galleries on Merseyside.

Printed by Birkenhead Press Limited,
1 & 3 Grove Road, Rock Ferry,
Birkenhead, Merseyside L42 3XS.

ISBN 0 9516129 0 5

Acknowledgements

So many people have helped in the production of this booklet that it is a rather invidious task to select names for inclusion here. Without the support of the Merseyside Development Corporation the work would have been impossible, and Graham Trewhella, who wrote the "Epilogue", has been a constant source of help and advice. The staff of the Liverpool Record Office and of the Municipal Research Loans Service have been very tolerant, as have the Inter-Library Loans Staff at the Sidney Jones Library. The Liverpool City Engineer's Reprographics Section provided artist's reference material by some subtle plan-copying.

The inclusion of the magnificent Robert Salmon painting is the result of a very timely "tip-off" from Professor Thomas Murray of Yale University and of the ability of Michele Butterfield, at the Portland Museum of Art, to get a transparency to me much faster than I had any right to expect.

Among my Museum colleagues mention must be made of David Ryan and his staff at the Maritime Record Centre who developed their physiques by locating and producing many hundredweights of documents. The whole of our Photographic Department laboured to produce quality prints from unpromising material. Samantha Ball has dealt with difficult and sometimes fragmentary sources to produce the line illustrations, and Sandra Page compiled the index as well as reprocessing the text to correct my errors, omissions and changes of heart. Any errors which remain are mine alone.

Of Countyvise, and particularly John Emmerson, I need say no more than that we entered into this partnership with them largely because of their genuine interest in local history. We have not been disappointed.

CONTENTS

Merseyside Portfolios

Merseyside Portfolios is a joint imprint of the Trustees of the National Museums and Galleries on Merseyside (NMGM) and Countyvise Ltd, set up to produce a series of occasional booklets on subjects in the history of Merseyside's Dockland.

The work is being done by the Port Survey, a small research unit within the Merseyside Maritime Museum which operates with substantial financial assistance from the Merseyside Development Corporation. Its key responsibilities are to assess the historical importance of sites and buildings within the MDC's Designated Area, to ensure that anything of importance is adequately researched and recorded, and to publish the results wherever these may appear to be of reasonably general interest. The booklets are intended to be accessible and "readable" whilst retaining quite extensive bibliographies and notes for the scholarly user.

The task of producing the first two booklets proved both easier and harder than had been expected. It was easier in that the enormous archival resources of NMGM reduced the amount of field recording and measurement needed by furnishing contemporary descriptions, and often drawings, of virtually everything surviving on the ground.

We also found, however, that much more checking of historical sources than we had anticipated, would be needed. Repeatedly errors were found which had passed from one previous historian to another over long periods. In the case of Princes Dock, for example, the starting date of the construction is normally given as 1816. It was Picton, writing more than a century ago, who confused the laying of the foundation stone with the actual start of the works. It is clear from the Docks Committee Minutes that the works started not later than 1811, and indeed a little may well have been done in 1810.

On the Birkenhead side, we found repeated reference to a report of 1828 by Messrs Telford, Stephenson and Nimmo which formed the first scheme for docks on the Wirral side of the river. Robert Stephenson was at this time working flat out in Newcastle on the design

5

and construction of steam locomotives: the man who went surveying in Wirral was the less eminent (though very competent) Robert Stevenson of Edinburgh. Sulley, writing in 1907, actually transcribes the report spelling Stevenson correctly, but twice "corrects" the spelling to Stephenson when commenting on it.

The enforced re-checking of original sources has had the benefit of bringing to light evidence disregarded by previous writers who have tended to produce a rather anodyne view of the development of the docks as the product of an unusually lively class of entrepreneurs reacting to favourable economic circumstances. In real life, of course, they were not a class, they were individuals, some good, some bad, some clever, some stupid.

The intention of the booklets is primarily to record the history of the structure extant at the time of the survey. We hope, however, that in going a stage further to tackle the problems of why and how they were built we can not only make a contribution to the overall history of the Port, but also point the way for further work in an area of study where much yet remains to be done.

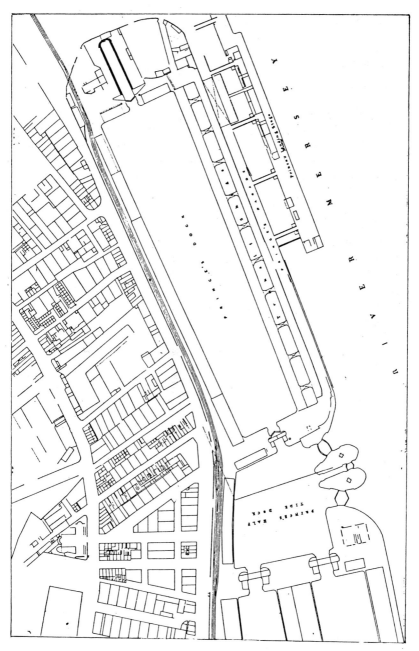

General Site Plan. Source: 1891 Ordnance Survey.

Conception and a Lengthy Gestation

In the first full year of trading after Liverpool's first dock opened its gates to traffic, some 27,200 tons of shipping used the port, showing a useful growth to reward the enterprise of its citizens in building the first commercial wet dock in the country. With the occasional stutter brought about by wars, financial panics and such irritations, trade continued to grow throughout the eighteenth century, the tonnage reaching, for example, 68,100 by 1759 and 324,100 in 1789.[1] From the 1780s the rate of growth had been accelerating rapidly, and because of Liverpool's location away from the main theatres of trouble, the French Revolutionary Wars strengthened rather than weakened Liverpool's trade.

This could only lead to pressure for more dock space, and in 1799 an Act of Parliament was obtained to authorise the building of a new dock to the South and of the first to be built to the North of St. Nicholas' Church. On 4th December that year, the Common Council[2] resolved that the advice of 'some eminent civil engineer' be obtained on the subject of 'the two Intended New Docks'. Christmas jollifications were obviously briefer in those days, for by 10th January the Council had not only agreed terms with an eminent civil engineer, they had agreed a fairly specific brief for him and a great catalogue of questions on which they wanted his advice.

The man they had chosen was William Jessop, the most prolific of all canal engineers. His name is little known today outside of the limited circle of canal historians, and does not get even a passing mention in the *Dictionary of National Biography*, although one of his pupils, Thomas Telford, rates $5\frac{1}{2}$ pages. The blame for this strange situation lies with that doyen of biographers, Samuel Smiles, who frequently appropriated to his subjects, of whom Telford was one, the works of other engineers. Subsequent biographers have followed Smiles' choice of subjects with an astonishing unanimity, with the result that there is but one biography of Jessop,[3] published in 1979, long since remaindered and out of print. Only by reading that book is it made clear that Jessop was a great engineer, and that his obscurity is posthumous: during his lifetime he was undoubtedly eminent and his services were greatly sought after. It is highly doubtful if the Common Council could have found another man as good.

The sixteen questions put to him included 'would he recommend One Dock of 400 or 500 yards in length in preference to two smaller docks?', 'does he approve of forming a straight line of embankment (or as near as conveniently can be) from South to North' and 'would he build it so far to the Westward as below Low Water Mark at Ordinary Tides?'. There was also a slightly naive enquiry whether he could 'recommend a Mode for Building the Dock Walls that will be secure and permanent, the present walls being very subject to sink and in other respects give way?'[4]

This slight mishap between the Wars had the benefit of providing us with a good impression of how an eighteenth century river wall was built.

Relatively few engineers would put forward a proposal for a wall without claiming that it would be secure and permanent. Jessop's report was dated 4th April 1800, and advocated the building of a single large dock. He did not approve of building his long straight embankment below low water mark, for he considered that this would considerably and unnecessarily increase the cost, so that the new dock would be quite long and narrow. The stone walls would, naturally, be 'of an improved construction'. He also proposed the building of a substantial half-tide entrance basin with single gates to the river and further gates to the dock. It thus served as a giant entrance lock, but also provided usable quay space provided that the river gates were opened only when there was sufficient water for craft berthed as well as for those passing in and out. The new dock should have a passage from its south end through to the George's Dock, so that vessels could pass through from the new dock to the older ones without having to lock out into the river. This related to his fears about silting: he specifically warned against the use of tidal entrance basins and felt that even half-tide entrances should be used only when necessary. A tidal entrance basin has no gate to the river, the water entering and leaving with the tide. It acts simply as an area of sheltered water provided to facilitate manoeuvring vessels into the entrance of the dock proper, and Jessop's fears were fully justified when the eventual Princes Basin suffered silting problems. Indeed both Jesse Hartley and G.F. Lyster[5] would have done well to heed his warning. He clearly recognised that the new dock should be capable of taking in larger vessels than those already in general use, insisting that the entrance must be 'sunk at least 3 feet lower than the present sill of the George's Dock'. It may be mentioned in passing that he made uncomplimentary remarks about the shallowness and proneness to silting of King's and Queen's Docks, the two most recent additions to the system.[6] The new North Dock was not only to be deeper, but some 50% larger in area than the largest opened to that time. It was a farsighted and ambitious project intended not only to keep pace with rising demands, but to move ahead of them, by building a real 'state of the art' dock. All that was lacking was the money to build it. The Dock Trustees were heavily in debt from previous ventures, notably King's Dock,[7] which was the largest to date and had only been completed four years, and raising capital in time of war was not easy. The war effort also served to drive up the price of labour and of a number of materials required, notably wood. Above all, like every war from the First Crusade to the First World War, it required large numbers of horses both for combat and for transport and a continuing supply for the replacement of the large numbers killed. Horses played a crucial part in heavy earth moving, and their availability in large numbers at reasonable prices in time of war was highly unlikely. The Common Council did not own all the land required for the new dock, and there were considerable problems in some of the acquisitions, notably that of the old Fort which stood near the north end of the site. The Peace of Amiens does not seem to have made the slightest difference, probably because relatively few people expected it to last even as long as it did before war broke out again.

Trafalgar effectively removed the French Navy from the Seas and almost completely annihilated the Spanish. Napoleon's 'Continental Blockade' was so effective against Liverpool that the tonnage of ships entering Liverpool and paying dock dues rose by nearly 50% between 1806 and 1810[8] and signs were at last emerging that Napoleon was not invincible on land. In short, the revenues of the Port were better able to service loans and optimism about the ultimate course of the war might make loan capital more readily available.

These happier circumstances did not mean that everything was marvellous on the Dock Estate again. On-going maintenance competed for funds, and although details are lacking it would appear that errors had been made in the design of both Queen's and King's Docks, since alterations were made to the sluicing arrangements of the former, while the latter was deepened and widened, as well as having its west pier extended.[9] A need for economy, if not downright parsimony, may, therefore have been the reason that a report from John Rennie was commissioned in 1809. A clear and demonstrable reason for not proceeding unquestioningly on the basis of Jessop's report was that there was still hope among the members of the Docks Committee that it would be possible to avoid the problem of acquiring the site of the Fort. Rennie's report established that there was no way to build a dock of radically different shape from that which Jessop had proposed.[10]

The man who would take charge of the works was John Foster, who had been appointed 'General Surveyor and Controller of the Works' in December 1799. He was responsible for just about everything, including all works and workmen and the examining and signing of all bills and accounts. He was not, however, a specialist harbour engineer, and it was understood that Rennie could and would be called in from time to time. Under Foster came the Clerk of the Works, who was responsible mainly for checking quantities, measurements and weekly bills. The management team was completed with a Foreman each for the Carpenters, the Stonemasons and the Labourers. Foster, being in charge of all the works of the Dock Estate, and also Surveyor to the Corporation, clearly could not give all his time to the works at the New North Dock, and the responsibility must have been a heavy one for his Clerk of the Works.

There does not appear to have been a formal 'start date' on the works, which is perhaps hardly surprising in view of the gestation period of ten years, but by early 1810 things were beginning to happen. The supply of stone from the old local quarries, at St. James Mount and Brownlow Hill, for example, had long roved inadequate for large new works on the docks, and for Prince Dock, as elsewhere, stone was brought in by sailing flats from Runcorn. Clearly there was serious work afoot by March 1810 for by then the Runcorn Quarrymen felt secure enough to write to Foster informing him that they could not continue to supply stone at the present price and that they must have an increase of $\frac{1}{2}$d per cubic foot (to $6\frac{1}{2}$d). The Docks Committee agreed this, but it was obviously not a complete solution, for shortages of stone continued, and in May Foster was authorised to advertise for additional supplies of stone, or to hire a quarry, rock, stock and barrel.

This work seems in some ways to have been a little premature, for it is clear that the committee did not know exactly where the money was coming from, and they certainly did not have detailed plans of all the works. Nor did they own all the necessary land. The degree of uncertainty which remained is revealed in the Heads of the new Bill to go before Parliament seeking extension of the time limits in the 1799 Act, additional borrowing powers and variations in the size of the Dock. The first version, discussed by the Docks Committee on 13th June 1810, was a "Plan X" for a dock which could be built without the acquisition of the Fort site, leaving its width about the same (300ft at the South end and 250 ft at the North) but reducing its length, though not to less than 1,000 ft. A second version, discussed on 13th October,

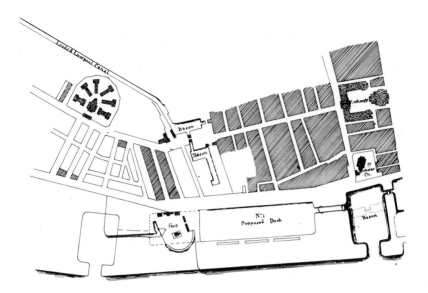

William Jessop's plan of 1800 (dotted line) and John Rennie's 'Plan X' for a dock which would not require the site of the fort. Source: Deposited Plans, Dock Act of 1811.

still envisaged a much reduced dock of just over six acres. The most important provision of the Bill, however, appeared to be that which changed the basis of charging dock dues from being on the tonnage of the vessel only to being on tonnage both of the vessel and of the goods. It was thought at the time that this would bring about a rapid rise in revenue to an estimated £60,000 p.a., but the unfortunate outbreak of the American War meant that this figure was not to be achieved until 1815. The petition was sent to Parliament on 22nd January 1811, and on 7th February, Foster was authorised to claim expenses for his forthcoming trip to London to give evidence to the Commons Committee. On 12th June Aldermen Case and Earle returned from London with the news that the Bill had been passed, to be rewarded with a vote of thanks for 'their unwearied zeal and assiduous attention during the tedious progress of the Bill'.

If any particular start date for the works at Princes is sought, it must be this Act which triggers it. What can be said with certainty is that Picton's start date of 17th May 1816[11] is an example of the common error of confusing the ceremonial laying of a foundation stone with the mundane business of starting work. Whatever work may or may not have already started, on 2nd July 1811 the Docks Committee Resolved and Ordered 'That the Surveyor be directed to take immediate measures for commencing the building of the Southernmost of the Northern Docks and that the said dock be in future called and known by the name of The Princes Dock'. Large purchases of stone had been going on for over a year and notice to quit had been served on the tenants of part of the site in the previous November. A steam engine had been acquired, for the same meeting gave Foster authority to arrange the erection of 'the Steam Engine lately received from Messrs. Bateman and Sherratts of Manchester for hoisting and discharging stone and for other purposes'. This was, of course, the high-tech solution to the problem of scarcity of horses. The horse-power problem had been given an additional twist by the extremely high prices current for virtually all basic foodstuffs which was causing widespread hardship to the poor. The result was that horses became extremely expensive to feed – if they could be obtained anyway – and that a good deal of moral opprobrium attached to feeding to horses anything which might be eaten by people. In December 1811 a public meeting was held to raise a subscription for the poor, and shortly afterwards at another meeting a number of prominent local figures deposited substantial sums on loan to the Dock Trustees specifically to enable the employment of extra men through the winter on the dock works and a further £2,000 was raised to be distributed in charity. The following April a committee appointed to buy up provisions for sale at reduced prices to the poor specifically urged those who kept horses to feed them as little as possible.[12] Once again, we can see some urgency and some risk-taking evident, for the plan was still for the smaller version of the Dock, which was clearly not what the Committee wanted or intended to build, but only by proceeding on that basis could a start be made. The work which had been going on thus far, site preparation and work on the wall on the inland side, did not represent a commitment to either scheme, but it did represent a commitment to build something. As early as August 1811 these works were obviously reasonably advanced, as Foster was authorised to start work at the North of Princes Dock to provide temporary accommodation for the coasters which had been displaced from their normal beaching spot around what is now the avenue to the East of Princes. Perhaps a greater risk was that not all the money required was lined up, and on 21st December 1812 it was resolved to seek a Government Loan of £50,000 for the completion of the Dock. The same Petition and Bill would seek authority to acquire the Fort, thus allowing the Dock to be built to the original intended size. There is no formal indication of serious lack of money included in the Minutes, but it may well be significant that the last payment for stone which the Committee had authorised was nearly six months previous.

If the passage of the 1811 Act had been tedious, this one would be more so. It was not unopposed (the Leeds and Liverpool Canal Co., for example, objected to the clause allowing the Dock to be entirely walled around) and from the fact that Foster's expenses in London were almost exactly ten times what he had incurred in 1811 we may deduce that a good deal of lobbying needed to be undertaken in addition to the formal giving of evidence.

It may be, however, that we should not set too much store by these expenses, as it appears that Foster had other business in London at the time. He was trying to secure a slightly dubious grant of arms for himself[13] and may also have been involved in attempting to negotiate the sale of a collection of Greek marbles acquired by his son.[14]

It was not until 22nd June that the Bill went through; news of its passage was enthusiastically received in Liverpool and rapidly followed by a request for the payment of the first £20,000 of the loan.

Although the work had slowed down on the site, the project had not ground to a halt, and two particularly thorny problems had been solved in the meantime. The Common Council had approved the transfer of the Fort and provided a loan of £5,000 and Rennie had produced the design for the River Wall, the most critical and difficult of the works required. A second steam engine had been acquired and 'infrastructure' works like the diversion of the Bath Street Sewer had continued. The management of the works had been strengthened by the appointment of Foster's son, William, as his assistant at the substantial salary of £250,[15] establishing a tradition which both Hartley and Lyster would follow, not necessarily uncontroversially. The scheme was now over thirteen years old, and it had only just arrived at the point where it had the detail designs, the land and the money to carry into effect what was really quite similar to Jessop's proposal of 1800. Surely nothing further could go wrong.

One further thing had already gone wrong, namely the outbreak of the American War in 1812. Liverpool men had for years lobbied the Government to try to prevent the disputes over the rights of neutral shipping coming to the point of war, but in the event the consequences were less disastrous than had been feared. Liverpool's tonnage had reached a record level of 734,400 in 1810, which dropped to 446,800 in 1812, but from 1813 onwards it recovered steadily.[16] The ability to service the loans for the new dock had been impaired, but not destroyed, and building could, and did, go ahead as planned.

By September, Foster was spending serious money, including £839 1s 10d on timber and in November he was authorised to provide iron railways and wagons for carrying spoil, the wagons to be drawn by the same steam engine which was employed in 'excavating and removing the earth'. In January the payment of £927 19s 0d for oak was authorised; this was for the cribwork of the foundations of the river wall. But amid the quickening of the pace, there remain traces of indecision. The railway, for example, was apparently abandoned by a decision of 18th May 1816, yet on 19th June the same year a payment of £782 0s 4d to Thomas Dove[17] for the supply of 'road rails' was approved. The extra steam engine was found to be insufficient and a very much larger one was ordered from Boulton and Watt for £1,125 3s 0d.[18] The works were being carried on by a slightly odd combination of direct labour employed by Foster and his team with contractors taken on to complete specific aspects of the work. Whilst this may have seemed a natural thing to do when the Surveyor was used to undertaking major projects with his own labour force but had insufficient men for a scheme of such size as this, it rather flew in the face of the accumulated experience of the canal industry which had, collectively, far more expertise in the undertaking of such works than any other.[19] We should not be too surprised if some things did not go quite as intended. It has been said, of course, that Foster had outside family business interests which were not compatible with his position as Surveyor. Whilst these suggestions had some foundation beyond the undoubtedly correct legal proprieties on which they were offered, there is no firm evidence to establish that they worked to the physical detriment of the building programme.

1816 saw the economy move in favour of the Dock Committee and its works. The tonnage through the port, which had been recovering since the trough of 1812, reached a new record figure of 774,200 tons. More important, however, was the unemployment and poverty which awaited Wellington's returning heroes.

By November, it was clear that serious efforts in Winter Poor Relief would be needed again and a public subscription to pay wages to extra men taken on to Foster's direct labour pay-roll was proposed. On 14th November Foster was authorised to proceed with the building of the 'Basin at the North End of the Princes Dock' if the subscription proved sufficient. There was a certain amount of argument as to the best arrangements to be made for the subscription and it was eventually decided that it should take the form of substantial interest-free loans to form a fund of not less than £20,000, the income from which should be spent 75% on wages and 25% on materials. Liverpool business men being both rich and generous, it took only two weeks to pass that target, and on 2nd December it was reported that employment could be offered at a reduced wage of 2 shillings per day (equivalent to the going rate for agricultural labourers) to between 500 and 600 men. Preference was to be given to men with families to support and to those who had lived in Liverpool for at least six months. To cope with this influx, Foster was authorised to employ extra supervisory staff, and to purchase an extra flat[20] for the use of the stonemasons.

Work must now have accelerated considerably, for the following month another flat was purchased, and in March the old problem of the Fort was finally laid to rest by the payment of £3,975 for the vacant possession. The small barracks attached to it was used on a temporary basis for accommodation for superintendents and foremen living on the site. The River Wall must also have been making significant progress, for the Committee discussed the question of mooring the Floating Baths[21] against it. The wall was not complete – a minute of 21st November 1817 describes it as 'now building' but clearly its southern end must have been well advanced. The entrance passages were nearing completion: oak for the gates and iron heels for their heel-posts were authorised respectively in May and November 1817. The saga of the on-off-on railway continued with the authorisation of a payment of £1,609 5s 11d to the famous ironmaster, William Hazeldine, for 'tram roads and waggons'. Another addition to the 'muckshifting' equipment was the purchase of a large number of secondhand wheelbarrows from the recently completed Leeds and Liverpool Canal for no less than £267 8s 0d

An idea of the problems facing dock constructors can be gained from the sad story of an Iron Swivel Bridge for the south entrance of the Dock. Foster was authorised to contract for this on 21st November 1817 and on 23rd December 1817 it was noted that he had agreed with Messrs. Aydon & Elwell of Bradford, who had previously supplied iron cranes and similar items for the works, at a maximum price of £1,400. By July 1819 repeated badgering of the supplier had produced no bridge, and Foster was directed to 'repair to Bradford'. In March the following year the Solicitor was set the task of getting them to supply, again without success. In May 1820 desperation had set in, for Foster was authorised 'to apply to the two ironworks recommended to him by Mr. Rennie ... and to contract with one of them upon the best terms he can'. Clearly the answers he got involved a certain amount of pursing of lips and sharp intakes of breath, for on 29th June the Solicitor was 'instructed to take legal measures for enforcing the contracts for the erection of the bridges by Messrs. Aydon & Elwell' but this attempt must have proved ineffective as well for in September William Hazeldine entered into an agreement for the supply of the bridges for the North end of George's Dock and the south end of Princes for the sum of £1,187 10s 0d payable in cash.

As the twentieth anniversary of the obtaining of the original Act for the Dock approached, anxiety was mounting. On 27th May 1818 it was resolved 'That the Surveyor do proceed with all possible dispatch to finish the basin at the North end of the Princes Dock ... in order to provide with the utmost expedition additional dock space which is at this time so very much wanted'. This exhortation came on top of the granting of quite substantial ex gratia payments to various loyal servants who were working all hours of the day and night to achieve 'all possible dispatch'. On 13th January, for example, £10 0s 0d had been authorised for Thomas Dealy, who had the considerable task of dealing with the wages of all the extra labourers. There also appears to have been an increase in the accident rate, presumably occasioned by haste. No figures have been recorded of the exact numbers of accidents, but the Dock Committee had a charitable fund which dealt fairly generously with those injured or the families of those killed. There is a definite increase in such grants, and there are also entries for payments to men variously described as 'worn-out' or 'broken-down in their health' which appears to be the formula used for those who had been effectively disabled by working all hours in all weathers in the winter.

Since at least 1805 it had been a fixed policy that Princes Dock should be entirely walled round in the interests of security. This was not only aimed at the sort of petty pilferage which had always gone on at open quays, but also at more ambitious frauds and evasions of duty. In July 1813 the works were sufficiently advanced to allow the building of the perimeter wall to begin along the east side,[22] and agreement was reached with the Surveyor of Highways as to the width of the road, and the arrangements for its paving and maintenance. The last of the tenants on the west side of Bath Street were given notice to quit in December, to allow the completion of the wall. It would be some time, however, before the entire site was walled – the wall at the south end, for example, was only approved by the committee in August 1820, a year after it had proved necessary to employ three watchmen and offer a standing reward of £5 to informers to prevent 'the depredations, especially at the Princes Dock, by persons stealing the brass bushes out of the cranes and other hoisting machines and also rope ...'[23]

There was another, more insidious, security problem. The project involved quantities of materials and numbers of men quite beyond the previous experience of the management, and as suggested above, insufficient heed was probably taken of the experience of others. Compared to the sort of regime enforced by men like Jessop or Telford, the system was wide open to abuse, and abuse was exactly what it got. When it became clear that large-scale fiddling had been going on, the Audit Commissioners (who were appointed under the various Dock Acts) began an investigation into the purchase and control of materials. Their initial report, dated 28th December 1822,[24] indicated that there had been considerable over-charging for a number of items, particularly legal services, ironwork and lead. The most serious item, however, and the only one which after further investigation could be found to have no possible reasonable excuse, was the supply of stone. Under a contract with William Hetherington made in September 1815, almost £200,000 had been paid for stone. In relation to a price of a few (old) pence per cubic foot this was an amazing sum. The amount of stone represented would have more than sufficed to sink each and every one of the vessels said to have delivered it. The fraud might possibly have remained undetected had the malefactors had the decency to pay Dock Dues on the amount they claimed to have delivered rather than on the much smaller amount that they actually had delivered.

There was much more to this fraud than fiddling by the masters of the flats and by the men who measured the stone when it was discharged. Although the threatened prosecutions were quietly dropped, there is little doubt that this was the cause of the extraordinary resignation of John Foster and his two principal assistants only three days after the appointment of Jesse Hartley as Assistant Surveyor.[25]

But while the fraud was continuing, it was not slowing down the works, only increasing their costs. During 1819 the first buildings round the dock and basin were erected, including two sheds and an office for H.M. Customs, a weighing machine house and a wholesale fish market. By April 1820 the Dock was sufficiently near completion to allow the appointment of John Talbot as Superintendent and Director of the vessels and craft using the North Basin of Princes Dock and the following month the Committee considered a request for berths for steam vessels in the Dock. This was granted, on the slightly onerous condition that they put out their fire before entering.

The great day was drawing nigh. The pressure of trade meant that the new Dock and its entrance basin were put into use on an ad hoc basis as soon as possible, but that was no reason for foregoing a junket of gargantuan proportions. The choice of date was highly symbolic: it was the day of the Coronation of King George IV, deliberately chosen to provide the opportunity for a display of mercantile loyalty to the 'wronged' Queen Caroline. It was, in short, a symbolic gesture by the more Radical and Whiggish Liverpool Men who chose to use the opening of the Dock as a grandstand for a thumbing of the

Radical Nose to the traditionally Tory class of Freemen of the Town. The welcome accorded to William Cobbett in November 1819 had not been a flash in the pan, for the very issue which he used to consolidate Radical support on a national scale had been kept on the boil ever since then, to be brought noisily forth on this occasion. The *Liverpool Mercury* did not miss its chance:

'It will be seen in another part of our paper, that we declined acting with the Coronation Committee in this town, but we have to record, and we do it with pleasure, the gratification we experienced in joining with our fellow-citizens in the ceremonies of opening the Prince's Dock (sic).'[26]

The ceremonies must indeed have been impressive. Most of the quayside of the dock had, as yet no buildings on it, so that nearly $^3/_4$ of a mile of quay was available for spectators, who were drawn up in highly organised groups. At the south passage were the Mayor, Common Council, Dock Trustees, merchants, brokers and gentlemen of the town with, facing them across the water, three companies of infantry, gentlemen on horseback, gentlemen dismounted, two heralds, a champion in a suit of armour[27] and the Blue Coat Boys. Around the dock were seemingly endless trade and friendly societies interspersed with further companies of the military and numerous bands. The number attending was estimated as exceeding the total population of the town – perhaps as many as 80,000 – and in addition to the large numbers round the dock, every vantage point overlooking the site was crowded with onlookers clinging onto St. Nicholas' Tower, on various roofs and on 'every wall, mast, yard or crane'.[28] At 12.00 the gates of the dock were opened, and the East Indiaman *May* entered the basin, but had to wait almost an hour before the tide rose sufficiently for her to enter the Dock proper. To constant cheering and the reports of pistols fired in the air, more and more vessels entered the dock, including the steam packets which 'were full of well-dressed company', flats, rowing boats, a three-foot model topsail schooner and Mr. Kent's Marine Velocipede. Happily, Public Address systems yet lay long in the future, so there were no speeches.

At 1.00, the various groups set out for the procession, led by the champion and of such length that it took 'above an hour to pass any given point'. The various trade societies were all attired or equipped in a manner to indicate their calling: the Glassmakers 'wore hats of glass, with glass feathers, and each carried a glass sabre'. The Carters appear to have been popular: 'in their new frocks, with whips in their hands (they) looked like honest sturdy John Bulls and were cheered accordingly'. After the procession the serious free-loading got under way, on board ships, in inns, taverns, hotels and club rooms and, of course, in the evening there was a grand dinner at the Town Hall, with another less grand one at the Liverpool Arms Hotel. The Liverpool Mercury's hack was disturbed long into the night while writing his account by loud and probably slurred protestations of loyalty to Queen Caroline echoing round the streets as the various dinner parties broke up, 'but in as much as we sympathise in the feelings which elicited them, we are gratified in having been thus constitutionally disturbed.'[29]

The opening of the dock was a considerable achievement for the drive and enterprise of the Liverpool merchant class. It had been built at a time when construction of any major work was exceedingly difficult, but its progress had been doggedly pursued for over 20 years. When work could proceed in one direction or another it did, if it could not, then it was left to wait, but left without any question that it would be resumed as soon as possible. This faith in the future was in one sense remarkable: Liverpool had lost the slave trade on which it was popularly supposed to rely heavily, and it had faced a war with a country which was its most important single trading partner. It had prospered through the Continental Blockade, and scarcely noticed the loss of its once-prosperous whaling trade. By 1823, the tonnage liable for dock dues exceeded one million, and it continued to grow, reaching 1.5 million in 1831. In that growth, Princes Dock, having the largest water area and the best entrance played a vital part. Its success proved that even in bad times there was great scope for growth, and it would have been surprising had its opening not been followed by some minor improvements, a short breathing space – and the building of more docks.

KEY TO DOCK NAMES

1. Seaforth Container Terminal. Royal Seaforth Docks.
2. Gladstone Dock and Branch Docks Nos. 1 & 2.
3. Hornby Dock.
4. Alexandra Dock and Branch Docks Nos. 1, 2 & 3.
5. Langton Dock.
6. Brocklebank Dock and Branch Dock.
7. Canada Dock and Branch Docks Nos. 1, 2 & 3.
8. Huskisson Dock and Branch Docks Nos. 1, 2 & 3.
9. Sandon Dock.
10. Sandon Half-tide Dock.
11. Wellington Dock.
12. Bramley-Moore Dock.
13. Nelson Dock.
14. Stanley Dock.
15. Collingwood Dock.
16. Salisbury Dock.
17. Trafalgar Dock.
18. East Waterloo Dock.
19. West Waterloo Dock.
20. Princes Half-tide Dock.
21. Princes Dock.
22. Canning Dock.
23. Canning Half-tide Dock.
24. Salthouse Dock.
25. Albert Dock.
26. Wapping Dock.
27. King's Dock No. 2.
28. King's Dock No. 1.
29. Queens Dock and Branch Docks No. 1 & 2.
30. Coburg Dock
31. Brunswick Dock
32. Toxteth Dock.
33. Harrington Dock.
34. Herculaneum Dock and 4 Graving Docks
35. Cammell Lairds Fitting Out Basin.
36. Morpeth Branch Dock.
37. Morpeth Dock.
38. Egerton Dock.
39. Vittoria Dock.
40. East Float.
41. West Float.
42. Bidston Dock.
43. Wallasey Dock.
44. Alfred Dock.

General Dock Plan

Robert Salmon, American, 1775-1842, OPENING OF PRINCE'S DOCK, LIVERPOOL, by the Mayor R. Bullin, Esq., Escorted the Lancashire Light Horse, 19th July 1821, oil on canvas, stretcher: 15 x 22", Portland Museum of Art, Portland, Maine, Bequest of Howard K. and Alison McEldowney Walter, 1985.

The Opening of Princes Dock

At first sight this painting by Robert Salmon appears a little conjectural, and another Salmon painting survives which is almost identical but purports to depict a completely different occasion. The wooden drawbridge is not mentioned in documentary sources.

However, the scene tallies closely with the newspaper accounts of the opening of the dock, including the weather conditions, and it is perfectly possible that the drawbridge was a temporary expedient made necessary by the problems encountered in obtaining the iron swing bridges. There was, at the time, no other location on the docks where any similiar view to the river could be seen.

The Buildings of the Dock

The euphoria of the opening faded fairly rapidly. At the meeting of the Dock Committee on 23rd July 1821, it was resolved that a payment of 10 shillings per week be made from the Charitable Fund until further notice to 'William Gerard, hurt in firing the salutes upon the opening of the Princes Dock'. Perhaps more indicative of the scale of the remaining problems was the authority granted to the Surveyor to build privies on each side of the Dock: it might have been expected that these would have been completed ready for the opening of the Dock. The fact of the matter was that all that had been opened was a dock with one entrance: few of the buildings around it had even been started and the passage to George's Dock was incomplete. In April the following year it was necessary for the Committee to instruct Foster to get moving on this south entrance. In November, a bond holder named Myers wrote enquiring when repayments of the debt on Princes Dock would commence, and the Committee's response was that 'Princes Dock is yet so far from being complete that it is not in the power of this Committee to give any response to his enquiries'.[30]

It is very difficult to put a total price on the building of the Dock. Although payments made on its account were supposed to be separately entered, this was not always done, and hundreds of separate payments made over a period of at least 25 years create a picture of some confusion. It is also clear that the 'Princes Account' in so far as it was adequately separated, was 'milked' to provide at least materials,[31] if not contract services as well, for works on other docks. The figure which Picton quotes, of £650,000 is probably on the low side, but even that figure is about ten times the cost/acre of King's and Queen's Docks. The Dock Committee was not having trouble finding things on which to spend money.

There were further pressures on money as well. The continuing rise in traffic during the building of Princes Dock made it clear that, large and splendid though it was, the new dock would not long suffice to contain all the vessels wanting to use it. In particular, it was clear that the steamship, whilst still a bit experimental, had a great future, and one in which Liverpool wanted a stake. That posed problems beyond the simple questions of water space, for Liverpool had a very

29

cautious policy on precautions against fire. This was hardly surprising, as the town had seen some particularly disastrous fires in and around the Docks, of which the Goree Warehouse fire of 1802 was only the most famous, but the policy brought a risk of losing out on the steam trade. At first, steam vessels were only allowed into the docks if they drew their fires before entering and left under sail, lighting up when they were safely out in the river. Since superior manoeuvring ability when docking was among the more significant advantages of steamers, this was a requirement unlikely to stimulate trade. A sensible compromise appeared to be the building of a new dock, separate from the others, which would be specially for steamers. The building of such a dock (which would eventually be called Clarence) was discussed as early as 1st August 1821, and it was resolved that first steps towards obtaining an Act for its construction should be taken. This, it should be noted, was before any consideration was given to the building of sheds or warehouses at Princes. The Act which eventually followed in 1825 also included powers to build what would become Brunswick Dock and to modernise the oldest part of the Estate. It enabled the increase of the debt to £1,000,000 which was sufficient also to allow the implementation of the controversial power granted in the 1811 Act to fill in the Old Dock.

The original intention had been for Princes Dock to have warehouses built round it in the manner later adopted at Albert Dock. In Liverpool at the time, warehouses could be roughly divided into three categories: those owned by large concerns for the storage of their own goods; those owned by specific warehousing undertakings which let space to anyone who needed it and, exceptionally, warehousing of a special nature built by the Corporation. In general such warehouses were off the Dock Estate, the only significant exceptions being the warehouses at the Dukes Dock (not at this time technically part of the Dock Estate) and the Public Tobacco Warehouse at King's Dock. Clearly the building of warehouses at the side of the largest and most modern dock in the town would threaten serious damage to the business of the warehouse owners, and their opposition to such a plan was concerted, emphatic and successful.[32] One cannot but suspect, however, that with such heavy commitments recently discharged and with other equally expensive ones envisaged, the Dock Committee was less than heartbroken at being forced to abandon its plans for warehouses at Princes. In hindsight, we may suspect that both they

Timber roof trusses of early nineteenth century style. These examples survived until 1990 and are known from field sketches, measurements and photographs.

and the warehouse owners were wrong and that the even greater competitive edge which the proposed warehouses would have given the port would have made *everyone* richer, but the decision was a sensible one at the time.

What was not sensible, however, was to leave the new 'flagship' dock lacking even the most basic weather protection for cargoes during loading and discharging, sorting, consignment and Customs inspection. The merchants, underwriters and shipowners of the town petitioned the Dock Committee about this highly unsatisfactory state of affairs, as a result of which the Committee resolved on 25th January 1822 to build four transit sheds, two each side of the Dock. They were to be open sheds of what was becoming a more or less standard type, with cast iron columns supporting wooden trusses and a planked and slated roof. Not only were there no side walls, but even the sailcloth screens used on some open sheds to diminish the effects of horizontal rain were absent. The response to this resolution was not exactly rapid either. By May, payment was made to Thomas Dove, ironfounder, for columns for these, but since the amount was only £13 3s 10d we may assume that all that was paid for was either pattern-making or the supply of a few sample columns. Thomas Dove was one of the suppliers suspected by the Audit Commissioners of gross overcharging, though the case against him was not finally proven, and in the end when his partner's father was no longer Surveyor, he did not get the main contract for the sheds.[33]

By August, Foster was ready for the construction of the trusses, and payment was authorised for two separate orders of 'Dantzic Balk' totalling £552 8s 6d. There now follows a prolonged and unexplained silence on the subject of sheds at Princes, only broken on 23rd March 1824 when the Surveyor was required to produce plans for sheds round Georges and Princes Docks. Foster was at this time in poor health and under severe pressure. His Superintendent of the Dock Works, Leonard Addison, had been barred from signing off bills and accounts for payment on 5th November 1823, but when Addison appealed to the Common Council and was allowed to make his case to them, it was not for the removal of this stigma that he appealed but for 'reinstatement'. No reason for Addison's suspension is given, but it is perfectly clear that he was heavily implicated in the improprieties which had dogged the construction of the Dock.[34] In August 1823 the

Dock Committee had resolved that it 'be recommended to the Trustees of the Docks and to the Common Council that the Persons to be appointed as Civil Engineer and Deputy Surveyor under the Surveyor be distinct persons and that they be not concerned directly or indirectly in any Trade,[35] nor in any other occupation whatsoever *saving that of an Engineer and Surveyor'*. The words italicised are, most unusually, written in the Minutes in red ink.

The day after Foster was authorised to produce his plans for the sheds was the day set for interviews for the new appointment of Assistant Surveyor, and that same day it was made clear that Addison, who had applied, was considered ineligible under the terms of the previous minute. The job was given to Jesse Hartley. Three days later Foster resigned, through the extraordinary procedure of his son sending a letter to the Committee announcing as accomplished fact, not as a proposal, his father's resignation. There were also received more conventional letters of resignation from Addison and from Heyes, Foster's Measurer of Dock Works. The depth of suspicion and ill-feeling may be judged from the fact that the man who had presided over the greatest expansion of the Port to date was allowed to resign by proxy without a word of thanks or comment being minuted by the Committee.

The plans which Hartley drew up have not survived, but the sheds which were built are shown in plan view in Nicholson's Survey of 1827 and may be taken to be of similar structure to those originally proposed, since Hartley continued to build open sheds on that principle for many years.[36] Even before Hartley's appointment, the attempt to prevent recurrences of the corruption and incompetence evident during the building of the Dock had led to the Committee resolving that in future an Agreements Book should be kept, wherein would be recorded details of all contracts entered into. From this we learn that Thomas Dove was displaced in favour of the Horseley Coal & Iron Co., and that the carpentry and slating work went respectively to Henry Griffiths and Charles Ammes. In 1836, Hartley produced his first Annual Report, and appended to it was a summary of all the expenditure for which he accepted responsibility since his initial appointment, including the cost of these sheds at £12,614.

In the early years of the Dock it had mainly handled goods from the United States, of which the only item liable to heavy duties was tobacco. Even that, being far from ready for use was not at such serious risks of smuggling or pilferage as, for example, wine or spirits. However, as new docks opened to the North, the American trade gradually moved from Princes, the steamers going to Clarence, the passenger packets to Waterloo along with much of the general merchandise, and the timber going to Brunswick. Princes became increasingly the centre for trade with the East and West Indies, China and South America. The goods in these long-haul trades tended to be very valuable – they had to be to make it worth carrying them so far – and often to attract high rates of duty. The result was that the old open sheds, even with their outer curtain wall, were no longer satisfactory. We may deduce from the amount of time and money that the Dock Committee spent on its constables and lock-ups from 1824 onwards that this problem did not appear overnight, but as with the building of the first sheds, expansion of the dock system tended to starve minor improvements, however needful, of money and of the time of the Surveyor's department. What was undoubtedly needed was secure transit sheds, but it was not until 1841 that the expenditure was tacked on to the Act of Parliament which authorised the enormous works completed in 1848. One of those works was the building of Bramley-Moore Dock, which would more or less complete the destruction of the US trade at Princes.

Some of Hartley's drawings of the 1843 sheds have survived. They were built on the West side of the Dock, behind a continuous open shed stretching the full length of the dock. The relationship between that open shed and the previous ones is unclear – none of the dimensions in relation to the dock itself tally, but equally it appears that some parts of the old structures were re-used. It was the rule more than the exception for transit sheds to be dismantled rather than demolished in order that their columns and trusses could be re-used; and indeed in some cases complete sheds were removed from one site to another with apparent nonchalance. The new open shed was 1,457 ft. long and 30 ft. wide[37] – significantly, the same span as the original sheds, though their total length had been only 1,215 ft.

The new secure sheds were relatively small. Their roof span was of 50 ft., and they came in three 'standard' lengths of 70, 125 and 140 ft.

Artist's Impression of the 1843 secure transit sheds on the West Quay. Sources: 3 drawings signed by Jesse Hartley, photographs of alterations in 1895 and 1929, field sketches and photographs of remains in 1990.

Referring to these sizes as A, B and C, the 11 sheds were symmetrically arranged ABBCBCBCBBA and were robust little brick structures. Despite several extensive re-builds of the west side of the dock, fragments of these sheds still remain incorporated in other structures revealing four-course walls of local brick in English Bond. The corners were radiused and the foundations of one of these radiuses survive. Several doorways, some door fittings and a number of roof trusses enable the formation of a surprisingly clear picture, considering that the buildings were obsolete by 1870 and have been heavily worked over four times since then.

The buildings which we see in this reconstruction are no longer transit sheds in the original sense of the term. They look like toy warehouses, and they are designed for storing goods for days rather than hours. Their doors have the double staple and hasp intended to carry two locks, one for the owner of the cargo and one for the Dockmaster, which betoken short-stay storage, rather than transit.

During this time, the entrance basin seems to have been devoid of any permanent buildings. It was variously used for the landing of fish, for small miscellaneous coastal cargoes and for movements of materials for the improvements to Princes Dock proper as well as for the building of Waterloo and Clarence Dock. This is indicative of the problems of tidal entrance basins; whilst they were almost as expensive to construct as a fully enclosed dock, they did not lend themselves to any settled trade involving anything but the smallest vessels. It was for this reason that, when the redevelopment of Waterloo Dock to provide a specialist grain facility was considered, Princes Basin was seen as ripe for conversion into a half-tide dock. In this new form, with the triple entrance which is still visible today, it was re-opened in 1868. To North and South were single pairs of gates for half-tide use, whilst in the middle, between two Hartley-style granite 'islands' was a lock which enabled flats and other small vessels to enter or leave at more or less any state of the tide. It was to these small vessels that the new half-tide dock became attractive, and the first specialised building on its quays was a railway transit shed completed in 1875. This was part of a system of berths spread throughout the dock system for the interchange of traffic between the railways and the large numbers of flats which transferred goods between Liverpool, Birkenhead, Garston, Ellesmere Port and Runcorn, with occasional sorties further

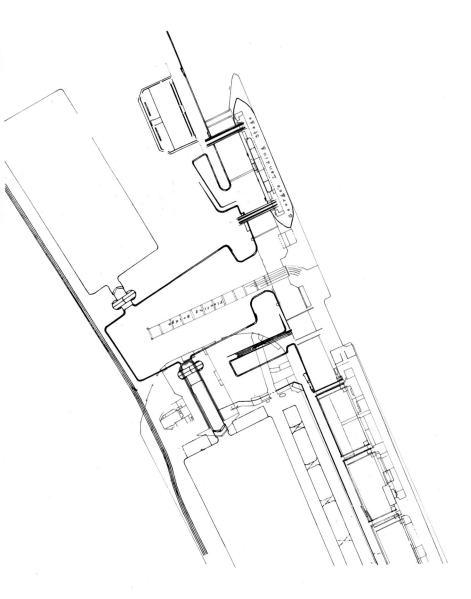

Composite plan showing the reconstruction of Princes Basin as Princes Half-tide Dock, completed, 1868. Sources: Ordnance Survey 1848 and 1891

afield. It was obviously a successful development, as by 1877 the 'raised Shed' on the East Quay was being extended by 129 ft. (some 50%) and a short-life wooden shed on the South-east Quay was added the same year.

The east side of the dock proper appears to have remained much as it was, but on the West side there were developments afoot. In 1878 'the old open shed on the West Quay has been taken down and re-placed by one of a lighter and more convenient character, 1515 ft. in length and the paving of the Quay, as well as the Coping of the Dock has been for the most part taken up and thoroughly repaired'. These works cost £9,103 7s 4d, and the adjoining (secure) transit sheds received extensive repairs to the value of £632 8s 8d.[38] This was not the first occasion on which the soft stonework constructed during the happy days of Foster's 'special relationship' with Messrs. Hetherington & Grindrod had been found wanting, for as early as 1860 'The old

The 'New' open shed of 1878 gets altered out of recognition in 1929.

Soft Stone Coping of the East Wall of the Dock being very much worn has been taken down and replaced with Granite'.[39]

By this time Princes Dock was totally obsolete in terms of the ocean-going vessels for which it had been constructed. Its entrances were still only 45 feet wide, and it still had an entrance depth over the sill of only about 17ft. (high water neap tide) to 24ft. (high water spring tide). These dimensions were pitiable in terms of the size of ships now used in the trades originally envisaged, but such was the momentum of growth in shipping movements that berths at Princes, so far from being shunned as obsolete, were the subject of acrimonious wranglings between the Board and the owners of smaller vessels wishing to use the Dock. In 1880, for example, Sandbach Tinne, a firm with long traditions in the West Indian Trade asked, not unrea-

Half-tide entrances can have their problems! A slight miscalculation leaves the full-rigged ship J.C. Boynton in an embrassing position, caught on the ebb.

sonably, for preferential use of the (obsolete) secure transit sheds for vessels of theirs landing cargoes of rum.[40] Such treatment was not guaranteed, because there were plenty of other shipowners still using quite small vessels in highly lucrative ocean trades. Whilst Sandbach Tinne were operating one ship of 1,748 tons, their smallest ocean-going vessel at the time was of only 125 tons,[41] a figure comparable with some of the larger cross-river grain barges.

The result was that pressure for change, both in the dock itself and in its buildings was largely ineffective. Why should the Board spend money on improving facilities which people would still fight over, when it had more pressing matters like forming a North Entrance that worked to occupy its mind?[42] So not very much was done to Princes Dock for quite a long time.

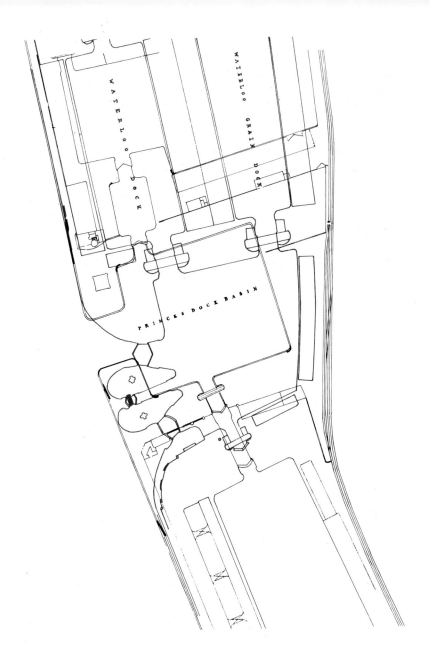

Composite plan showing the alteration of 1872-4, including the building of the Graving Dock. Sources: Ordnance Survey 1848 and 1891.

The triple entrance at Princes Half-tide after the 1868 alterations.

The Tower Building, Princes Half-tide Entrance, with two Mersey flats in the foreground.

A Change of Direction

The 1870s and 1880s were a turbulent time for the Dock Board. The new north works, including Alexandra and Langton Docks were an undertaking of unprecedented size even by the standards of the Board, and at the same time the rather haphazard South Docks system was being heavily reconstructed and modernised. In the middle lay a little cluster of docks which time had left behind. In the normal course of events it was to be expected that the Board would get round to them fairly soon and upgrade them, as had been determined for Brunswick Dock and everything southwards. However, matters were not as simple as that, for the new works at both ends of the Estate did not progress smoothly or quickly. Enabled under an Act of 1873, they continued until 1888, amid allegations of incompetence and corruption. Certainly the plans for more than one of the Docks were subject to major changes while construction continued, and the new entrance based on the old Canada Basin proved so unsatisfactory that it had to be reconstructed again by 1895. These problems came immediately on top of the belated completion of heavy investment in solving the inherited problems of the Birkenhead Docks, a programme which had dragged on until 1878. Whilst critics attacked the Engineer and/or the Works Committee, it is also clear that the Board was failing to determine and act on any coherent long-term policy.[43] The prospects for Princes Dock were not good.

An entirely separate problem had arisen which was to make a considerable difference to Princes Dock. Road access to the floating stages had long been difficult, with Georges Dock, Georges Dock Basin and the passage to Princes between the stages and the town. The short bridges to the stages sloped so sharply at low water that driving horse-drawn vehicles down to the stage varied between exciting and impossible on spring tides. The solution lay in the infilling of the passage, which allowed the construction of a long pontoon bridge, colloquially known as the Floating Roadway. Reaching inland for 550 ft., it kept gradients much more reasonable, and made vehicular access to the stage possible at any state of the tide. It also presented the opportunity to provide a wide approach road to Princes Stage, but required extensive alterations to the south boundary wall of Princes Dock. In the programme of work between 1872 and

The Floating Roadway at low water.

1874, the wall was not only rebuilt mostly on its present line but was also given a distinctly decorative appearance with a 'stone' balustrade matching the one which used to grace the sides of the passage for the floating roadway. A little of this balustrade still survives, its heavily weathered condition testifying that the superior qualities attributed to Frederick Ransome's Artificial Stone in his patent No. 877 of 1872 were largely imaginary. When new, it must have looked rather fine.

Built into, and forming part of, the boundary wall, is a small building with fancy iron grilles on the windows, which is the only obvious reminder of the main alteration to Princes Dock under the programme. The end of the infilled passage was converted into a small drydock suitable for the use of vessels of the type using the main dock, and the small building was its pumphouse. Inside was a mechanical lash-up which scarcely did justice to the nicely detailed exterior. The pump was of the chain type, with wooden 'floats' in wooden boxes, which was certainly all one was entitled to expect in a rather second-rate graving dock, since the first of the new high-speed centrifugal pumps to be used in Liverpool Docks did not start work until 1875.[44] The chain pump had, after all, the advantage of being entirely self priming, so that it neither needed to be built down a deep and expensive hole nor to be equipped with an auxiliary priming pump. Its tolerance of abrasive particles and small debris in the water it pumped was much higher than that of more high-tech machines. What was wrong with this one was what drove it. Mounted on blocks, with its outside fly cranks removed, stood the ancient railway locomotive Lion, built for the Liverpool & Manchester Railway in 1838. Its aged wrought iron boiler was still in service, still working at the L & MR's 'standard' steam pressure of 50lbs, set as the limit for the contestants in the Rainhill Trials of 1829. The steam cut-off was fixed at 81%, and this, coupled with the low pressure, made the thermal efficiency abysmal. A very ordinary small stationary engine of 1872 would have worked at about 100lbs with a cut-off of about 30-35%, using at the outside, one half of the weight of steam. The only thing to be said for this arrangement was that its first cost was low, and that it would eventually prove to be the means of survival of what is today one of the most important preserved locomotives in the world.[45]

The floating stage now consisted of a single structure uniting the former Princes and Georges Stages, and this, together with the improvements to the approaches, began to coax increasing numbers of passenger vessels out of the docks. Its palmy days as the home of the great Atlantic Greyhounds still lay in the future, but the implications of far reaching changes at Princes Dock were perceptible. Like the wholesale improvement of Princes, they would have to wait on more pressing problems.

Some of the problems at Princes were too acute to be shelved. The old secure transit sheds were too small and too much sub-divided for traffics which had grown a good deal since they were designed. For at least twenty years, continuous secure shedding had been recognised

The east walls of the 1843 sheds being supported while the side walls are removed in 1929 alterations.

as desirable, but it had not come to Princes. In 1882, HM Customs complained that the sheds were too dark, but on 12th March that year the Traffic Committee declined to lighten their gloom by fitting 'glass slates' as requested, and a further complaint in April 1885 was similarly rejected. The preferential use of the secure sheds for cargoes of rum (which some of the West Indies traders had sought) had been grudgingly agreed on 14th July 1880, but in April 1882 the concession was revoked because the pressure (and volume of complaints) from the general traffic was too great to allow of any space remaining under-used. What resulted was the gradual conversion of the sheds on the West Side into large clear-span closed sheds, though it must be conceded that the word 'gradual' is perhaps euphemistic. The West Sheds finally achieved the form in which they substantially remain today in 1929, the first steps having been taken in 1878.[46] By 1889, the first sliding doors were fitted on the quayside of the former open shed on the East Quay, together with continuous skylight of the type still

Ignore the foreground: the Board's photographer has unwittingly taken an excellent shot of the old south east shed which was not actually state-of-the-art by 1927.

visible in the surviving closed sheds. On the west side, however, no such improvements were made and users had to take their choice between a total absence of security and groping around in semi-darkness.

Such, however, was the pressure on dock space, that these primitive facilities remained much in demand. In particular, here as elsewhere, there was endless wrangling about appropriated berths. This system, whereby a berth is rented for the exclusive use of one shipping company, had been resolutely resisted by the old Dock Committee, and viewed with suspicion by the members of the new Board on its foundation. Their lack of enthusiasm for what seemed like a very easy way of putting money into the Board's coffers may well have been occasioned by a realisation that they would have to spend a great deal of time attempting to deal in an evidently fair way with the conflicting

A press of estuarial, coastal and ocean-going craft in Princes Dock about 1880.

claims of a seemingly infinite number of contentious customers. Even the old sheds at Princes (and the even older ones at Clarence) became the subject of long-winded and often bitter wrangles between several companies and the Board.[47] Two significant facts appear: the rival users were without exception occupied in the coasting trade; because of their competition, the Board was able to adopt an attitude where the renting of an extra 20 ft. of obsolete quay was seen as a gesture of great magnanimity. In the circumstances it is not surprising that the Board, which had problems enough with its big new docks (which were new enough but not big enough), could disregard its repeated promises to carry out a programme of general improvement at Princes. In March 1892 the promise was made that before any further large new works were undertaken, the obsolete central docks would be upgraded to provide first-rate facilities for the coastwise trade,[48] but the Act of 1898 was to be rather more concerned with large-scale extensions at Canada and Huskisson, together with major alterations

A rare view of Princes Dock 'as built' dating from about 1890. By this date the coasting trades were strongly represented, but 'Milton' traded to Brazil and there is another small ocean-going steamer in the background.

to King's and Queen's to put them back into contention for the ocean-going trades. Yet again, Princes languished, unloved and obsolete – but still in business. Baines quotes the total trade of Princes in 1858 at 215,474 tons,[49] whilst by 1899 the Belfast trade alone amounted to 155,819 tons.[50]

The long-awaited improvements finally arrived in 1904-5. One of the problems which had become increasingly evident, apart from the inadequacy of the sheds, was the shape of the dock walls. In the early days of dock-building, vertical stone walls had frequently burst from the bottom into the water, and the solution to this had been the building of walls with a batter of several feet, so that they were in effect an arch lying on its side. This was quite acceptable when the traffic was in sailing vessels of relatively small draught and with rounded

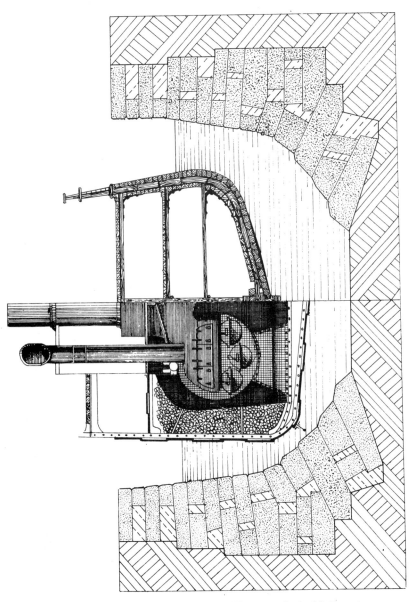

Composite Midshipsection of a typical sailing vessel of c.1840 and a steamer of c.1885 showing how the steamer can collide with a battered wall. Source: H. Paasch From Keel to Truck Antwerp 1885.

bilges. For deep, square-sided and flat bottomed steamers, often fitted with bilge keels as well, mooring against such a wall was inviting damage such as happened to SS Optic in 1899.[51] The solution to both problems lay in building out a new quayside on concrete piles, with new and spacious sheds on a concrete deck. The full length of the West Quay was so treated, and a concrete staging was built well out into the dock (some 50 ft.) at the south end to allow the building of a large new shed over the waters of the dock. The reasoning behind this was that as cargoes had grown larger, and methods of discharging more efficient, there was more need for usable quay space than there was for spare water space in which ships might await discharge, so that alterations tended always to increase the ratio of quay length to water area.

The new sheds were of an entirely different generation from those they supplanted. On the quayside were continuous sliding doors with a height of 16 ft., capable of offering an opening sixteen feet wide at

Silhouette drawing of the standardised steel trusses used in the 1904-5 sheds. Source: Field sketches and photographs, 1990.

The final phase of modernisation of the North Shed, west side, showing the cut-outs in the roof for the construction of the electric travellers.

any point along their length, or at several simultaneously. Their roofs had a clear span of 65 feet, and along the entire length of 600 ft. there were no columns, only one fire-break wall. To the 'avenue' side the doorways were again 16 ft. square. The slated roof had deep continuous skylights on both sides of the ridge, doubtless to the delight of HM Customs, and the buildings were good enough to be still serving the National Museums & Galleries on Merseyside at the time of writing.[52]

At the North end of the West Quay a rather more rough and ready solution was adopted. Again a concrete staging was constructed, which provided an area of open quay outside the 1878 open shed, but the conversion of the open shed and the remains of the old 1843 closed sheds behind into the clear-span closed shed which survives was what is nowadays called a phased programme. To put it another way, piecemeal improvised alterations were made over a period of an-

The enclosure of the old open shed made a fire-break wall necessary under the old Liverpool Building Acts; on the right a lone bricklayer is doing the job.

other 25 years. As early as 1901, the doorways and east walls of the old secure sheds 7 & 8 had been removed and the eaves (together with a few courses of brickwork) supported on girders and columns. Ultimately this solution was applied to the full length of what was to become the North Shed West Side, but as late as 1912 we still find reference to the addition of another three sliding doors.[53] By this time virtually the whole of the West Quay was appropriated to the Belfast Steamship Co., and it seems fairly clear that they were not too bothered about the condition of the North end, which they seem to have used rather in the manner of the old open sheds. Certainly they used a steam crane inside the sheds from 1889 but it was not until 1910 that ventilators were provided in the roof to allow the fumes to escape, which suggests a certain reliance on a substantial through-flow of air.[54]

*Princes Dock and the floating stage in 1930 or 1931.(The 1929
sheds are in use, but the 1932 passage dolphin is not.)*

In following through the sequence of events on the quayside, we
have passed by the main physical alteration to the dock in this period,
which was the building of Riverside Station. In the early 1890s it was
becoming clear that Liverpool could not expect to remain unchal-
lenged as the leading passenger port in the country or as the leading
emigrant port for a large part of Western Europe. Improvements to
the service offered were needed, and were made to excellent effect.
The floating stage was strengthened to allow it to take ocean liners
and the berths alongside dredged deeper. It was equipped with convenient and effective waiting rooms, customs facilities and baggage-
handling machinery. The vital step, however, was the construction of
a short length of railway down from the Waterloo Dock Goods Yard
to the West side of Princes Dock, and the opening there of Riverside
Station in 1895.[55] This brought main line passenger trains to within
70 yards of the ship's side and removed the need, at least for 1st class
passengers, to sample Liverpool's climate at first hand even for that

The old line of the corner of Princes half-tide is still clearly visible in this view of the new railway swing bridge in 1895 as is the 'tunnel' through the old shed.

short distance by roofing in Princes Parade and providing fully enclosed bridges to the floating stage at two levels.

When Princes Dock was designed, the railway industry amounted to a small number of horse-drawn tram roads and an even smaller number of colliery lines where pioneer steam locomotives of minuscule dimensions hauled four-wheeled coal wagons at little more than walking pace. The radius of curve needed to get the steam locomotives and coaches of the 1890s down to the river wall was far greater than could be achieved with the existing layout. To get the radii down to acceptable values, the extension to the Princes Half-Tide shed was removed, and a staging built across the south-east corner of the Dock. The passage bridge was removed and replaced with one which was not only much stronger, but which crossed the passage at an oblique angle, while on the far side another staging, across the

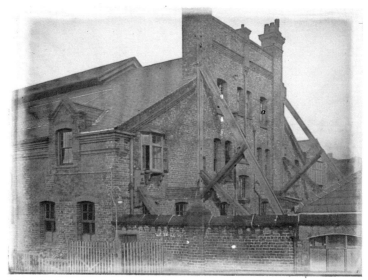

The old facade of Riverside Station, shored up after bomb damage in 1941.

north-west corner of the Dock maintained alignment for a curve which would take the track parallel to the river. Of course there was a shed in the way, but with the improvisation we should have come to expect at Princes, the track was simply driven through it in a sort of tunnel, leaving a rather odd-shaped offcut which was walled in and re-used.[56] It was also necessary to radius the end of the remaining portion of the old shed wall, and this alteration is clearly visible to this day. The track then ran between the old secure sheds and the boundary wall until it met the next problem in the shape of the curve needed to accommodate the points at the station neck. The west wall of the secure sheds was cut away and rebuilt with a curve, and a new end wall added.

The station looked marvellous. It had an impressive brick frontage with a bit of discreet terra-cotta ornament, albeit slightly obscured by a cluster of small buildings in front. The face to Princes Parade was nicely finished as well. Inside the train shed was fairly plain and simple, with light steel roof trusses and a very ordinary pitched roof, but with modest ornamental touches in the brickwork and quite a spacious feel to what was really rather a small station. Its beauty was only skin deep, for behind the ornament and the paintwork on its east wall lurked the old east walls of the 1843 sheds, much hacked and patched around. Its impressive west wall contained stretches of the old boundary wall of the dock, rebuilt on the cheap, using the old copings and footings of the previous wall, in 1853. This would not have been so bad had not the old wall had two courses of batter while the new wall was built straight. The Dock Board probably assumed, doubtless correctly, that passengers would have more to look at and think about than the precise alignment of the brickwork.

Whilst the station had noticeable effects on the physical layout of the east side of the Half-Tide and the west side of the dock proper, it

Cutting down the haunches of the Passage in 1929. The ledge on which the two men are working represents the amount of width gained at a ship's bilge.

had no direct effect on the actual trade of the dock and facilities needed for that. The availability of rail access on the West side of the dock was plainly an advantage, but one which was not immediately taken. In 1901, a series of doorways was formed in the east wall of the station to allow goods being loaded or offloaded via the adjoining transit shed, but the provisions of a direct siding into any of the sheds seems only to have occurred in 1928. Although Liverpool had never been in the forefront of rail transhipment, a wait of 107 years is somewhat above average.

The present range of sheds on the East Quay is the only building on the dock that really looks as though it was designed from scratch and built all of a piece. In fact this does the sheds at the South End, West Quay an injustice, for their rather scrappy appearance is the result of later modifications. However, the East Sheds serve to remind us that even the long-postponed programme of 1904-5 did not go all the way in modernising the dock for the coasting trade. Although the new works on the West Quay had been completed by 2nd August 1905, in September the dock was to be run dry to investigate the passage. The reason for this was that the steamers of the Belfast SS Co. were 'up to the last quarter of an inch that can be got into the Princes Dock',[57] as Alfred Holt explained to the Board on 16th November. A particular problem was that the passage had been built with an invert arch at the bottom, so that any deep square-bilged ship that was up to the full width at quayside level was at risk of wedging itself at bilge level. The decision was taken to cut the 'haunches' down square, but not to widen the passage. Exactly why this had to be done as a second bite at the cherry, when the dock had been drained for many weeks to put in the quayside pilings is not explained, but the seasoned dock researcher knows better than to expect otherwise. There had been complaints in 1891 which had resulted in a previous partial solution, and in 1909 the Engineer's Report enigmatically refers to the enlargement of the bridge dolphin[58] at the passage. This, of course, shows that vessels had been at least leaning on, and at worst colliding with, the swing bridge in their efforts to get through the inadequate passage.

In 1894 a fire broke out in the East Sheds which destroyed some 475 ft. of their length. It might have been expected that this would provide the stimulus to design a new and modern shed, but in fact all

An MDHB loco makes light work of a little demolition work on the old East Side Sheds, using a cable, a snatch block and a bollard.

A selection of plant, ancient and modern, is in evidence as joiners (centre) wearing flat caps and waistcoats work on the concrete shuttering for the deck of the 1929 East Shed.

This view of the piles of the 1929 East Shed under construction also gives a good impression of the original wall of the dock.

View below the 1929 East Shed, showing the piles and decking.

This study in sunlight and shadow shows the rudimentary access equipment still used in 1929. Through the door the Tower at the Half-tide entrance is clearly visible.

The new east sheds nearly complete in 1929.

that happened was that the damaged part was reinstated in a slightly altered form. It was only in 1889 that the East sheds had been equipped with doors (and then not for the full length of the quay) and continuous skylights, but perhaps more indicative of the primitive facilities offered was the fact that only then had the floor been laid with asphalt truckways. Prior to this, the floors had been entirely laid in setts, which have two great advantages: they provide excellent grip for horseshoes and they are very durable. As a surface for the use of hand trucks they multiply the tractive effort needed by a factor of several and greatly increase the risk of damage to goods by their falling off the truck. This work was evidently deemed sufficient to keep a Hartley open shed at the technological cutting edge of the port industry for some decades more, for the 1905 programme passed the East Sheds by.

Almost finished: the Passage has been squared out, the new gates fitted and the swing bridge placed. But the brick patch in the old masonry (extreme left shows that only the minimum was done).

The Great War and the outstanding commitment to complete the Gladstone System meant that further improvements to Princes occupied their customary place in the queue for resources, but the situation was changed by the sale to Liverpool Corporation of the Clarence Dock for the building of their new power station. Clarence had, like Princes, been updated to a reasonable extent in 1904-5, and there were effective berths in regular use there. Of the £339,000 obtained for the site, almost half was applied to the Sinking Fund – a desirable step as the cost of servicing the Board's debt had risen by over 50% since the outbreak of war[59] – but the residue was sufficient to allow improvements at Princes as some compensation to the coasting trade for the loss of space at Clarence. The concrete piled quayside on the west side having proved successful, the East side was similarly treated, with authority being given on 14th November 1928 for Belfast SS Co. to move temporarily to West Waterloo while the work proceeded. In addition to the building of an entire range of new sheds on the east, the passage was to be widened and the north shed on the west side was to be modernised.

The new sheds were of thoroughly up-to-date design so far as single-storey sheds went. Their slender steel roof trusses were strong enough to allow the use of electric travelling roof cranes, and they were equipped with full length doors on the quayside, smooth and efficient asphalt floor, full-length skylights and even the luxury of electric lighting. On the landward side they had railway sidings running the full length as a 'passing loop' from the main line of the Dock Railway. They had not been a cheap job: the cost of steel reinforcement for the concrete alone was put at £19,731.[60]

At the north end, west side, the hotch-potch of alterations based on components dating back at least to 1843 continued, but with the vital difference that this time the result was a coherent shed with continuous skylights, continuous quayside doors, good large roadway doors, a railway siding running into it, two electric 'travellers' built into the roof and a nice new lithocrete floor, this last item alone costing over £3,000. Despite its antiquated origins, the only disadvantage this shed now suffered was the line of columns supporting the valley gutter.[61]

This programme of works seems to have achieved, rather belatedly, what was being promised in the early 1890's, namely a specialised and thoroughly effective centre for the coasting trade, with special reference to Irish traffic which had been the major user since then. As always, there were a few features which were not quite right at the first attempt, with alterations needed to the fendering in May 1930 but apparently only one significant problem. The widened passage had, of course, allowed access for larger vessels, and these were again finding ways of making contact with the swing bridge. Their destructive urges were thwarted by the construction in 1933 of the huge concrete dolphin still standing to the South of the East side of the passage. It seems to have been good enough until 1949, when the new swing bridge, replacing the one which had collapsed in 1945, isolating Riverside Station for three years, proved too tempting a target for the stern end of Ulster Duke.[62] Such misfortunes notwithstanding, all the evidence seems to support the Journal of Commerce's view that 'The most important new work undertaken during the year was the modernisation of the Princes Dock to suit the requirements of the Irish Trade ...'[63] There are some grounds for suggesting that prior to that date, work at Princes had often been aimed at satisfying a variety of requirements, but not necessarily those of the companies which used the berths.

The recession in the coasting trade which had followed the Great War began to lift in the mid-30s, and this, combined with the efficiency of the new facilities caused renewed pressure on berths at Princes. There were only two ways to increase capacity; either a part of the half-tide dock could be modernised or the old graving dock could be converted into a branch dock. The enlargement of Princes Passage and the continuing traffic in grain and oil seeds to East Waterloo Dock meant that the Half-Tide was increasingly needed as a 'vestibule' or turning area, whilst the marginal lengthening of the Graving Dock in 1911 and its re-equipment with new pumps in 1929 did not alter the fact that there was no shortage of old fashioned small graving docks in the Port. It was eminently dispensable, and in November 1938 the Journal of Commerce reported that a new berth formed by converting it into a wet branch dock had been put into service. The next year saw an increase of 23% in Liverpool's coasting trade.

Alongside this new berth, the former South Sheds, again bodged-up open sheds of Hartley vintage, were removed and the present south-west shed constructed. This is an interesting piece of improvisation, for although at first sight it looks like a completely new shed of similar design to those at the south end of the West Quay, its roof trusses are of the rather odd composite type used in the 'new' open shed of 1878 at the North end West Quay. They were obviously reclaimed from an older shed elsewhere on the estate, but the building which resulted was again a good unencumbered space and doubtless highly effective at the job for which it was designed.

The Second World War put Liverpool in the front line, and whilst the main weight of aerial attack was only fairly briefly directed at Liverpool, the damage done was very serious. Some two linear miles of transit shed were either destroyed or incapacitated; just one aspect

The 1926 Coastwise Passenger's Waiting Room, Princes Parade which took the Irish passenger trade out of the dock until the adoption of Ro-Ro car ferries.

of the huge reconstruction task when peace came. No very serious damage was done to Princes Dock itself or to its sheds, but Riverside Station was hit and put out of action for a short time. The present station front is an entire post-war reconstruction and shrapnel damage can still be seen on the walls of the South End West Shed and on the 'Stokers' Monument' on the far side of St. Nicholas Place. The coasting trade generally had been hard hit by the war, both physically in terms of ship losses and financially by loss of some of its markets. As a result, we find Princes Dock yet again at the back of the queue for new investment.

In 1949 the new Waterloo Entrance, which had been long planned and whose construction began before the outbreak of war,[64] was finally opened. This made the docking of Irish passenger ferries a practical proposition, which it had not really been in the days of the archaic half-tide entrance. The Coastwise Passenger Terminal was right at the North end of Princes Parade and consisted of a mostly wooden waiting room built in 1926 on the site of a former cattle pen. Its approach stretched well beyond the luxury of the overall roof of Princes Parade and involved a long and windswept walk huddled against the wall to keep under the rather narrow pavement shelter provided. The first steps in making the facilities a bit more civilised were taken in 1952 when Coast Lines gained a little land from the Dockyard which still lingered on at the South end of the Princes. They constructed a new gateway and Police hut, and a covered way from the gate to the shed which was to do duty as the terminal. The covered way was eventually found to be necessary as a bus shelter as the services to Riverside were run down in advance of its eventual closure in 1971. The new terminal, a rather ugly brick and concrete edifice grafted onto the South end of the 1905 sheds, was opened on 10th December 1954 with facilities, creature comforts and decor of a very much more modern and congenial kind. The Daily Post spoke particularly highly of the colour schemes.[65] This términal was, however, only for the Belfast Service: passengers for Dublin had already been catered for on the east side of the Dock in the previous year.

Slick and modern as these new facilities looked, not far beneath the skin lurked a fair amount of obsolete building and equipment. In 1952, for example, a small 'blockhouse' had been built inside the West Shed to house a converter – establishing that the electricity sup-

View from the Liver Building showing the infilling of the graving dock and the construction of the Ro-Ro facility, 1965.

ply was still on DC. In 1957, the Board's Docks and Quays Committee authorised the fitting of two T-type bollards at the northern part of the Coast Lines' West Side berth to render unnecessary the practice of tying ships to the piling of the quaysides! The shed roofs on both sides of the Dock were in poor repair; serious money was spent on the East side in 1958, and two lesser jobs were done on the west side in 1957 and 1958. The total cost was very nearly £15,000. A matter for much greater concern arose in 1960, when it appeared that the steel reinforcement of the 1905 concrete piling which supported some 7/8 of the area of the south sheds, west side was corroding. This condition can cause rapid deterioration and collapse as the corroding metal expands and bursts the concrete, and it must have been with some relief that the Works Committee heard on 25th March that only £3,000 worth of work was needed.

By the mid-60s the decline in rail freight and the rise in car owner-ship and average mileage was exerting pressure for conversion of fer-ries to Ro-Ro (Roll on Roll off) operation for carrying vehicles, and it was this pressure which led to the last new investment at Princes Dock. In 1965 the Board spent £81,000 on substantial improvements to the West Side sheds, including the strengthening and resurfacing of the floor, re-roofing, and the provision of a new electrical supply. Coast Lines shared in the project and undertook the construction of the RoRo ramp leading from the South West shed, the provision of two 7.5 tons portal cranes and a payment of £32,500 to the Board to relocate their dockyard to release marshalling space. In the event, the Board decided they could manage without relocating it, and could simply farm out its function to either the North or South Dockyards. This apparent bit of sharp practice was offset by the provision of extra space obtained by filling in the branch formed by the old graving dock, clearing away some redundant residences and resurfacing the area.[66] The total investment was little short of £250,000, and whilst some aspects of the work still showed the aged nature of the site and buildings, it was an effective facelift which enabled a convenient mod-ern service to be provided very close to the City Centre. By late 1966 the work was well advanced, and the new services were in operation for the summer season in 1967.

In this account there is one fatal pitfall. Little mention has been made of freight, and the new development was completed just at the dawn of the container revolution. No facelift of Princes Dock, on its long narrow site, however good, could make it effective for the hand-ling of containers. By 1969 B & I Line were operating container ves-sels and the same year the demise of Princes Dock was effectively sealed by the acceptance by the Board of a tender of £1,116,500 for the construction of a new ferry and coastal container terminal nomi-nally at Victoria Dock, but in fact also including parts of Trafalgar and West Waterloo. When the new development opened at the end of 1971, only one regular service remained at Princes, namely the Bel-fast service now managed and operated by P & O. This ceased in 1981, ending a history of 160 years of traffic in a dock which had slipped from 'state of the art' to obsolescent within its first twenty years and had never quite caught up since.

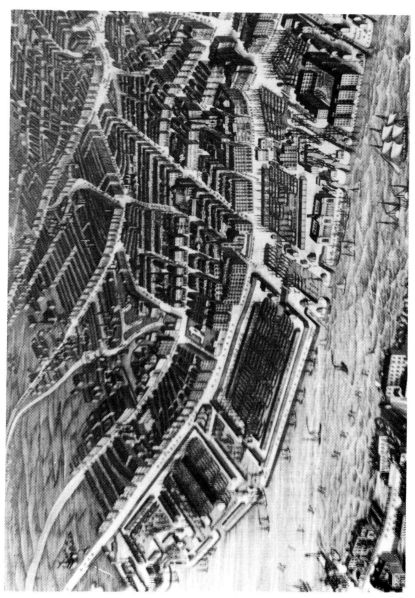

*Slightly fanciful Balloon View of Liverpool Docks about 1850. Was Princes Dock really **this** busy?*

Epilogue

With the occasional exception of small warships visiting HMS *Eaglet*, no ships have used Princes Dock for several years, and most of the site is in a decaying condition. Yet, situated on the river front immediately north of the Liver Building, and on the fringe of the City Centre it is not just an important site, but a strategic one. Clearly visible from the very busy Dock Road and conspicuous to the numerous tourists taking ferry trips in the summer, it is one of Liverpool's most public pieces of dereliction. As such it is highly damaging to perceptions of Liverpool and of central Merseyside and does nothing to inspire business confidence or investment. What a come-down from the day when the champion in a suit of armour led the procession in celebration of its opening.

Merseyside Development Corporation was established by the Government in 1981 with the primary objective of breaking the spiral of decay in which significant areas of the Merseyside Waterfront were locked. Rapid progress was made in the revitalisation of the obsolete South Docks, and in 1988 the MDC's Designated Area was extended to include, among other sites, the Central Docks, from Princes northwards to Nelson.

The objectives are fairly broadly based and centre on the creation of an improved environment for work, residence and leisure – and investment. However, as a short-term agency, MDC brings to these objectives a degree of single-mindedness and of urgency. It is able to concentrate its attentions on relatively small areas, and Princes Dock site, with its key location has a very special potential for the future. It is the best City Centre waterfront site remaining, which gives it an importance well beyond its own boundaries and also attaches a particular premium to 'getting it right'.

The Corporation's preference is for an office-led mixed development which makes use of the locational benefits of the site. Such a development should attract investment which would not come to Liverpool for any more run-of-the-mill opportunity, and the indications are that this will indeed be the case, as major developers in association with the Mersey Docks and Harbour Company as landowner, have shown considerable interest in its potential.

It is also important, though, that the new development, however beneficial its effects on the fortunes of the local business and commercial community, should be of a fitting nature for a site which will inevitably affect one of the world's great urban skylines. Perhaps as important is the retention of a sense of place in both space and time. MDC, as Planning Authority and Development Agency will ensure that the new development respects both the past and future. In the long history of Princes Dock this is the first time since the New Approach Works of 1873 that such considerations have troubled anyone's mind, which seems to offer some grounds for optimism.

Note on Sources

This booklet is based on two main groups of sources. The first is the evidence on the ground: Buildings, structures, ground surfaces and occasionally things below the ground. It was precisely because this evidence may be jeopardised by redevelopment of the older Dockland areas that the Port Survey was established, and the records made during the Survey will be lodged in the Maritime Record Centre. Merseyside Maritime Museum.

The second group is the enmormous archive of the Mersey Docks and Harbour Board, also housed in the Maritime Record Centre. It is probable that the history of no other Port is documented in such breadth and depth. The principal types of material used for this booklet are:

1. Minute Books. Fairly brief formal accounts of the Proceedings of the Board, of its Committees and its predecessor body the Docks Committee.

2. Worked-up Papers (commonly known as WUPs or UWUPs). Compilations of material, often over quite long periods of time, on specific subjects. These not only provide a good way into the Minutes, but may also be much more informative.

3. Drawings and photographs more or less speak for themselves. They provide valuable evidence of construction and alterations of buildings and machines.

4. Engineer's Reports. Beginning in 1836, these can be dangerous to accept at face value: they were prepared by the "insiders" for the consumption of the "outsiders".

The other sources used, whether in other archive collections or from previous publications should be readily traceable from the Bibliography and Footnotes.

Notes

1. Figures from F.E. Hyde, *Liverpool and the Mersey*, David & Charles 1971, Appendix 1.
2. The Common Council was, loosely speaking, the predecessor of the City Council. References to its decisions relate to the Dock Committee minute books.
3. C. Hadfield and A.W. Skempton, *William Jessop, Engineer*, David &Charles, 1979.
4. Dock Committee Minutes,'(hereafter DCM) , 10th Jan. 1800.
5. Lyster suffered serious and recurrent problems in his attempts to improve on Hartley's Tidal Basin at Canada Entrance. See my forthcoming paper on Harold Littledale in *Transactions of the Liverpool Nautical Research Society* for details.
6. Jessop's report is transcribed in DCM 1st May 1800.
7. For a detailed history of the Liverpool South Docks, see N. Ritchie-Noakes, *Liverpool's Historic Waterfront*, HMSO 1984 (hereafter LHW).
8. Hyde, *op.cit.*, Note 1.
9. LHW, p.37.
10. Rennie reported back to the Dock Committee on 14th August 1809.
11. J.A. Picton, *Memorials of Liverpool*, Walmsley, 3rd Edn., 1903 (hereafter Picton), p563.
12. Picton, p.294.
13. Gregson Papers, Liverpool Record Office, LRO 920 Gre 2/20.
14. Ibid, 2/23.
15. Common Council, 4th March 1812.
16. Hyde, *op.cit.*, Note 1.
17. One of Thomas Dove's partners was James Foster, son of John Snr. and brother of William.
18. Authority for payments was appended to DCM for each meeting.
19. Thomas Telford took George Stephenson to task for his unconventional (and not uniformly successful) management on the Liverpool & Manchester Railway: *Report to The Exchequer Loan Bill Commissioners*, 4th Feb.1829, in Telford Papers, Institution of Civil Engineers, ref T/LM 13.
20. A 'flat' was the characteristic Mersey sailing barge, the general

maid of all work on the river. After the introduction of steam towing, extensive use was made of dumb flats.

21. The floating bath was a vessel resembling a hopper barge, the 'hold' being open at both ends to allow the tide to flow through. It normally anchored in mid-river, but also required a mooring when not in service. Picton, p.326.

22. DCM 7th July 1818. *Gore's Annals* record the 'First stone of the Prince's (sic) Dock boundary wall laid' on 20th May 1813, but omit to mention where.

23. DCM 3rd August 1819.

24. MD&HB Collection, Volumes of Proceedings ref. 19/4.

25. DCM 27th March 1824.

26. *Liverpool Mercury*, 20th July 1821.

27. Quite an avant-garde move: it was two years before the publication of *'The Broadstone of Honour'*, the 'Bible' of neo-chivalry.

28. In spite of the Regulations, reproduced on the back cover of this booklet. It should be noted that the *Mercury's* estimate of the population of the town was well below the mark.

29. *Liverpool Mercury*, 20th July 1821.

30. DCM 15th November 1822.

31. Eg. On 23rd Aug 1822 (DCM) payment of a total of £552 8s 6d for 'Dantzic Balk' (oak) for the Princes Sheds was authorised, but when Jesse Hartley came to build the sheds two years later, this considerable amount of expensive timber was nowhere to be found.

32. Summarised in Picton, p.568.

33. It went to the famous Horseley Ironworks in the Black Country.

34. An abstract of title to the Birkenhead Ferry Hotel (Gregson Papers, Gre 3/9) indicates that Addison received a pay-off of property to the value of several thousand pounds from Hetherington and Grindrod, suppliers of stone & contractors for masonry work.

35. Foster Snr. still operated a substantial joinery and contracting business, as well as a sawmill. For further details of Foster's activities, see my forthcoming paper in *Transactions of the Historic Society of Lancashire and Cheshire* (1991).

36. LHW, pp.131-2.

37. MD&HB Engineer's Report 1877.

38. MD&HB Engineer's Report 1878.

39. MD&HB Engineer's Report 1860.

40. MD&HB Worked-up Paper No.83 documents this and similar disputes.

41. Figures from Lloyd's Register.

42. See above, Note 5.

43. For all of these problems, again see Note 5 above.

44. MD&HB Drawings, Princes 4/8 to 4/19.

45. A. Jarvis, 'Untwisting the Lion's Tale', *Railway World*, Vol. 41 No 477, January 1980 pp21-24.

46. The complex history of the alterations to this shed is detailed in the Port Survey files in MRC, and see below pp.51-53

47. MD&HB Worked-up Papers 17 and 83 give a wealth of detail.

48. MD&HB Discussions at the Board, 31st March 1892, and MD&HB Works Committee 6th November 1885.

49. Thomas Baines, Liverpool in 1859. Longman 1859. Part 2, p.96.

50. MD&HB Docks and Quays Committee Minutes (hereafter D&Q). 26th September 1899. This was an increase of over 30% since 1890.

51. D&Q 25th October 1899.

52. MD&HB Drawings, Princes 5/136 to 5/173.

53. These alterations mentioned in MD&HB Engineer's Reports for the appropriate years.

54. Details in MD&HB Worked-up Paper 180.

55. MD&HB Engineer's Report 1895.

56. See photograph, p.55

57. MD&HB Board Minutes, 16th November 1905.

58. A dolphin is an obstruction deliberately built to prevent vessels colliding with passage gates, movable bridges etc., when they are 'nested' in the open position.

59. S. Mountfield, *Western Gateway*, Liverpool University Press 1965, pp.147-8.

60. MD&HB Worked-up Paper 137: numerous entries from March 1929 onwards.

61. See photograph, p.46.

62. Lloyd's List 22nd October 1949.

63. *Journal of Commerce*, 8th November 1929.

64. *Jnl. Comm.* 18th November 1938 reported good progress and estimated completion within two years.

65. *Liverpool Daily Post*, 9th December 1954.

66. MD&HB Worked-up Paper P14, vol.2 gives full details.

Bibliography

J. Aspinall (pseud 'An Old Stager'), *Liverpool a Few Years Since*, Liverpool, 1852.

T. Baines, *History of the Commerce and Town of Liverpool*, London, 1852.

Liverpool in 1859, London, 1859.

R. Brooke, *Liverpool as it was during the last quarter of the eighteenth century*, Liverpool, 1853.

V. Burton, ed. *Liverpool Shipping, Trade & Industry*, Liverpool, 1989.

C. Hadfield and A.W. Skempton, *William Jessop, Engineer*, Newton Abbot, 1979.

F.E. Hyde, *Liverpool and the Mersey*, Newton Abbot, 1971.

A.E. Jarvis, *Hydraulic Machines*, Princes Risborough, 1984.

Docks of the Mersey, Shepperton, 1986.

S. Mountfield, *Western Gateway*, Liverpool. 1965.

'Liverpool Docks and the Municipal Commissioner's Inquiry of 1833 for Liverpool', *Transactions of the Historic Society of Lancashire and Cheshire*, Vol.115 (1963), pp.163-174.

J.R.B. Muir, *A History of Liverpool*, Liverpool, 1907.

J.R.B. Muir and E.M. Platt, *History of Municipal Government in Liverpool*, Liverpool, 1906.

J.A. Picton, *Memorials of Liverpool*, Liverpool, 1903, (2 Vols.), (3rd Edn.).

Braithwaite Poole, *The Commerce of Liverpool*, Liverpool, 1854.

P.T.L. Rees, ed., *Merseyside's Industrial Past*, Liverpool, 1990.

N. Ritchie-Noakes, *Jesse Hartley*, Liverpool, 1980.

Liverpool's Historic Waterfront, London, 1984.

H. Smithers, *Liverpool, Its Commerce, Statistics and Institutions*, Liverpool, 1825.

F. Spiegl, ed. *An Everyday History of Liverpool*, Liverpool, ND.

Ed., *Liverpool Packets*, Liverpool, No.2 and No.2+2. ND.

R.H.G. Thomas, *The Liverpool and Manchester Railway*, Newton Abbot, 1980.

Index